# Step by Step: Fault-Tolerant, Scalable, and Secure AWS Stack

Build and showcase a complete AWS stack. Develop skills in EC2, S3, RDS, VPC, IAM, CloudFront, Beanstalk & DynamoDB.

## Savitra Sirohi

# TABLE OF CONTENTS

# COPYRIGHT

# FROM THE AUTHOR

I am AWS certified (Solutions Architect - Associate level) and have over 20 years of experience in IT. I adopted AWS early, back in 2008, when setting up an AWS based SaaS business. As part of this project, I coached, for several years, a team of system admins and developers on this technology. For the last couple of years, I have been teaching a webinar based AWS solutions architecture course. This book has evolved from this long experience using and teaching AWS. I hope you will find it useful.

# AUDIENCE

In this book, you will use some of the most important AWS services, and build, step by step, a fault-tolerant, scalable, secure and easy to deploy architecture.

With its focus on implementation and skill development, this book is a good fit for you, if you are a developer, system administrator or a solutions architect who needs to use AWS in projects, or if you need to develop, and perhaps showcase, strong skills in this technology.

As you build the stack, you will also develop a deeper understanding of key AWS services, and of important architectural and security principles, and best practices. For this reason, this book is also good preparation for AWS certification exams, especially at the associate level.

# REQUIRED SKILLS

You will configure, deploy, and use a Linux (Ubuntu), Apache, MySQL and PHP app throughout this project. This book assumes you have some familiarity with Linux, SSH, vi (or similar) editors and with Git.

# INTRODUCTION

In this book, you will learn how to build a fault-tolerant, scalable, and secure stack on AWS. You will also incorporate ease of deployment. Fault tolerance is avoiding downtime, and avoiding data loss when something fails. Scalability is ensuring the same performance at higher loads by adding more capacity. At the same time, it is important to reduce capacity when load decreases, this to help lower costs. Security is protecting content and data from unauthorized access. Ease of deployment is the ability to easily and frequently update applications.

You will implement a complete architecture using AWS compute services - Elastic Cloud Compute (EC2) and Elastic Beanstalk, AWS storage services - Elastic Block Store (EBS) and Simple Storage Service (S3), AWS database services - Relational Database Service (RDS), ElastiCache and DynamoDB, AWS network services - Virtual Private Cloud (VPC) and CloudFront and Identity and Access Management (IAM), a security service.

You will need an app to build and verify the architecture and this book includes a simple PHP app. The app is typical, it manages sessions, has a database, and serves private content in the form of images, and as you work through the material, the app will help you understand architectural best practices for these typical app functions.

The architecture you will build is complex, so you will build it in small steps. You will start by deploying the PHP app on a single EC2 instance and then step by step, you will add fault tolerance, scalability, content security, ease of deployment and network security. Each step is a chapter in the book, and you will be able to work on a chapter independently of others. You will develop strong AWS skills as you work through these steps. In the final chapter, you will put everything you have learned together, and build a complete stack. The stack will be a concrete achievement that you can showcase in your resume, and talk about in your job interviews.

Before you implement a step, read the chapter's discussion section to understand what you will do and why. For instance, you will understand how EC2 auto-scaling groups help with cost efficiency, not just with scalability. Or how Elastic Beanstalk makes it easier to deploy application updates frequently. So, you will not just develop skills as you work on these steps, you will also gain a deeper understanding of architectural concepts and best practices, and of AWS services. For this reason, this book is good preparation for the AWS certification exams.

I hope you are excited at the prospect of developing serious AWS skills, building a concrete architecture that you can showcase and developing a better understanding of AWS services and of architectural best practices. Before you get started, take a moment to review the next two sections, the first on AWS costs, and the next on the PHP app you will use in this book. Good luck.

# AWS COSTS

You will need an AWS account to work on this project. Create a 'basic' account, this is one of four AWS support plans and the only one that has no monthly fee.

AWS offers a free tier - limited amount of free resources - for one year from the date you create your AWS account. The free tier is available for all the services you will use in this project, and you should make full use of it.

You must, however, inform yourself about the free tier limits, not all resources are free tier eligible. For example, always use t2.micro instances when you use the EC2 and EC2 based services such as RDS, ElastiCache, and Elastic Beanstalk, this is the only instance type that is free tier eligible. You will see a small cost when you use RDS multi-AZ deployment, this option is not free tier eligible. You will also need to create Amazon Machine Images, the cost of these will not be entirely covered under the free tier.

It is also important that you be disciplined, terminate or delete resources when you finish a practice session, even if these are free tier eligible. This is because you may consume your free tier credits and then start accruing costs. In the cloud, you don't have to keep resources running, because you can recreate them easily.

EC2 and EC2 based services are expensive, so terminate these resources as soon as possible. Services such as S3, CloudFront, and DynamoDB are serverless and accrue costs only when you use these services. You can retain these resources across practice sessions if you like.

In the first chapter, you will create an Amazon Machine Image, this Amazon Machine Image will contain the PHP app deployment that you will use throughout this project, I recommend you retain this Amazon Machine Image across practice sessions, this way you won't have to redo the app deployment. The Amazon Machine Image will cost you only about $0.80 per month.

AWS configurations don't cost anything, so don't worry about VPC, VPC subnets, VPC route tables, Internet Gateways, security groups, IAM roles, IAM policies, SSH and CloudFront key pairs. You can retain these throughout this project.

# PROJECT APP

You will use a PHP app throughout this project. The app has three basic functions - it manages sessions, it connects to a database and it serves private content in the form of an image. The app has a home page - index.php, and multiple PHP pages for each function:

* Sessions: session.php and dyn_session.php.
* Database: localdb.php, rds.php, rds_rr.php and memcached.php.
* Content: image.php, s3_image.php, cloudfront_image.php and signedurl_image.php.

The different pages for each function are simply different versions of the function, and you will use different pages for each function as you evolve the architecture toward its final state.

In chapter 2, High availability, you will use session.php, localdb.php and image.php. The session.php page stores sessions on the filesystem, localdb.php connects to a local MySQL server and image.php displays an image stored locally in the instance.

In chapter 3, Fault tolerance, you will use rds.php and s3_image.php. The rds.php page connects to a MySQL server in an RDS instance, the s3_image.php page displays an image stored in an S3 bucket.

In chapter 4, Scalability in app layer, you will use dyn_session.php, this page manages sessions in a DynamoDB table.

In chapter 5, Scalability in data layers, you will use rds_rr.php, memcached.php and cloudfront_image.php. The rds_rr.php page connects to an RDS read replica instance, the memcached.php page connects to a Memcached cluster and the cloudfront_image.php displays the image via CloudFront.

In chapter 6, Private content, you will use signedurl_image.php. This page displays the image via CloudFront, using signed URLs.

In subsequent chapters, you will use dyn_sessions.php, signedurl_image.php, rds.php, rds_rr.php and memcached.php.

# CHAPTER 1: DEPLOY APP

## Introduction

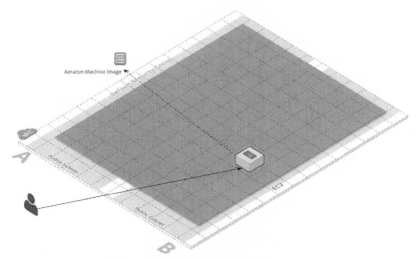

Figure 1.1: Deploy app and create Amazon Machine Image

**Objectives**
To deploy the project PHP app on a server, to inspect it, and to become familiar with it. You will also create an Amazon Machine Image of this server. You will use this image to create app servers, throughout this project.

**Key steps**
Launch an EC2 instance, deploy the PHP app, verify the app, create an Amazon Machine Image.

**You will learn about**
EC2 instances, Amazon Machine Images, AWS Regions, AWS VPCs, AWS Security Groups, EC2 instance types, and the AWS SDK.

# Discussion

You will use a LAMP (Linux, Apache, MySQL, PHP) app in this project. The app also uses the AWS SDK, a library published by AWS, to talk to AWS services such as DynamoDB and CloudFront. You will need to install these application dependencies - Apache, PHP, MySQL and the AWS SDK - when deploying the application.

The Amazon Machine Image is a template, it specifies the software that will be available on the instance that you want to launch. You will initially use the Ubuntu 16.04 image to launch the instance. After you deploy the application, and after you verify it, you will create an image of your server. This Amazon Machine Image will have the PHP app deployment baked into it and you will use it to launch an app server whenever you need one, you won't have to use the Ubuntu image after you create your own Amazon Machine Image.

Instances launched using this Amazon Machine Image will have the PHP app, you won't have to redo the deployment. This means you can terminate your EC2 instances when you finish a practice session, knowing that you can always re-create an app server easily when you sit down the next time to work on this project. Don't keep your EC2 instances running unnecessarily, this will eat up your free tier credits at the least and can sometimes result in significant costs.

## Implementation

Implement the steps below to launch an instance, to deploy and verify the app, and finally to create an Amazon Machine

Image. Before you start, here are some key points to remember:

## Region
When you are learning AWS, it is a good idea to use the North Virginia (US-EAST-1) region. AWS rolls out the latest features and services in this region first, and server costs tend to be lower as well. This region is hard-coded in a few places in the PHP app. If you don't use this region for your resources, you will need to change the app.

## Networking
Use the default VPC and the default security group for now. These are readily available and are configured for easy connectivity. In chapter 8, Network Security, you will implement better networking controls, for now, these will do.

## Instance type
Always use t2.micro instance type, this is the only instance type that is free tier eligible.

## Platform
Use the Ubuntu 16.04 Amazon Machine Image when launching your first server, the project app and the instructions in this book have been tested on this platform only.

## LAUNCH AN EC2 INSTANCE
1. Select 'North Virginia' (US-EAST-1) as the region.
2. Add a rule to the default security group, to allow SSH access to your instance:

| **Type** |
| --- |
| Inbound. |

**Protocol**
SSH.

**Port**
22.

**Source**
Anywhere (0.0.0.0/0).

3. Add another rule to the default security group, this time to allow access to the server via HTTP:

**Type**
Inbound.

**Protocol**
HTTP.

**Port**
80.

**Source**
Anywhere (0.0.0.0/0).

4. Launch an EC2 instance as follows:

**Amazon Machine Image**
Select Ubuntu 16.04.

**Instance type**
Choose t2.micro.

**VPC**

Use the default VPC.

**Security Group**
Use the default security group.

**Other Configurations**
Use default values.

**DEPLOY APP**
1. Use the instance's public IP address to SSH into the instance.
2. Clone the app into the instance using the git clone command.

```
# run this command after you SSH into the server, you will be in the /home/ubuntu folder
git clone
https://savitras@bitbucket.org/savitras/aws-course-php-app.git
```

3. Inspect the app folder and app pages.

```
# change to app folder
cd aws-course-php-app/

# list app pages
ls

# inspect the home page
cat index.php

# inspect the session page
cat session.php
```

```
# inspect the image page
cat image.php

# inspect the localdb page
cat localdb.php
```

4. Install app dependencies such as the Apache web server or PHP.

```
# run this script to install app dependencies, this script is
available in the app folder
# the script uses apt-get the Ubuntu package manager to
install software packages
sh apt-get.sh
```

5. Install the AWS SDK using Composer.

```
# install composer, composer is a PHP package manager
curl -sS https://getcomposer.org/installer | php

# install AWS SDK using composer
php composer.phar install
```

6. Copy the app into Apache web server's document root, so Apache can serve the app.

```
# copy php pages into the apache document root folder
sudo cp *.php /var/www/html/

# copy vendor folder (contains the AWS SDK) into the
apache doc root
```

```
sudo cp -r vendor/ /var/www/html/

# copy image to apache doc root, this image is used in the
image.php page
sudo cp aws-icon.png /var/www/html/
```

7. Exit the SSH session.

**VERIFY APP**

Figure 1.2: The app home page

1. Use the public IP address of the EC2 instance in your browser to test the app home page, like this - http://<EC2_INSTANCE_PUBLIC_IP>/index.php. Ensure the home page displays a 'hello world' message. You will also see links to other app pages.
2. Visit the 'Image in EBS volume' page (image.php), you should see an AWS icon displayed.
3. Visit the 'Local (EC2) session' page (session.php), enter your name in the form field and click ok, you should see a 'welcome' message.
4. Visit the 'Local (EC2) db' page (localdb.php), this page will display a 'failed to connect' message. This is fine, you don't have a local database server yet on the server.

5. Other pages also may not work fully at this stage, that's fine.

**CREATE AMAZON MACHINE IMAGE**
1. Select your EC2 instance and from 'instance actions', select 'create image'.
2. If you want to terminate the EC2 instance, wait for the image state to change to 'available' before terminating the instance.

# CHAPTER 2: HIGH AVAILABILITY

## Introduction

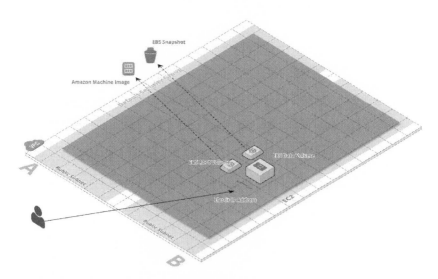

Figure 2.1: Highly available single instance architecture

**Objectives**

To develop high availability options for a single instance architecture. Specifically, you will develop recovery options for three types of failures - instance failure, storage failure, and availability zone failure. To also understand the limitations of the single instance architecture - that it is not possible to eliminate downtime and data loss, it is possible only to minimize these - this way, you will appreciate multi-tier architectures, the subject of the next chapter, better.

**Key steps**

Set up the app with a local database (a single instance architecture), prepare for failures, practice recovering from failures.

**You will learn about**

EC2 instances, Elastic IP addresses, EBS volumes, Amazon Machine Images, AWS Availability Zones. Also about the best practice of using separate root and data EBS volumes.

## Discussion

How will you make your single instance stack highly available? A single instance cannot be fault-tolerant, where a redundant set of servers and other components help ensure high availability when something fails. With a single instance, the best you can do is to recover from failures quickly.

If the storage volume fails, you will restore data from a backup into a new volume and replace the failed volume with the new one.

If the instance fails, you will create a replacement instance. You will move the storage volume from the failed instance to the replacement instance, so you have up-to-date data in the replacement instance as well. You will also need a way to point your domain to the replacement instance so your users' requests can be directed to the new instance.

If the availability zone fails, you will need to do both, restore data into a new volume and create a replacement instance. You will create the volume and the instance in a different zone. In AWS, availability zones are designed to be independent, if a zone fails, other zones are usually not affected.

It is a best practice to use a separate volume for application data, a 'data' volume. This way when an instance fails, you can easily detach the data volume from the failed instance and attach it to the replacement instance. Your instance will have two volumes, a root volume with the operating system, the application and its dependencies and the data volume with MySQL server's data.

You will need an Amazon Machine Image to create the replacement instance. And an EBS snapshot to restore data into a new volume. This Amazon Machine Image will create a replacement server with just the root volume, the EBS snapshot will help create just the data volume. In a real project, you will need to establish a process to regularly create Amazon Machine Images and EBS snapshots.

You will associate an Elastic IP address with your instance. In a real project, your domain will point to this IP address. You will be able to move the Elastic IP from the failed instance to the replacement, this will redirect your user requests to the replacement instance. Using Elastic IP addresses reduces downtime because you don't need to change DNS record sets to point to the replacement instance. DNS record sets are cached at the user end and changes to the record sets may not take effect immediately.

If the data volume fails, you will suffer data loss, as the snapshot may be several hours old. In all these failure scenarios, you will also suffer some downtime, this is the time you will take to create the replacement instance, to restore data into a new EBS volume or to reassociate the Elastic IP address. You can minimize downtime by scripting the recovery, but you cannot avoid it altogether in this architecture.

# Implementation

First, you will set up the single instance architecture by installing a local MySQL server on an EC2 instance, that already has your app deployment. Next, you will prepare for recovery by configuring a data volume for your MySQL data and by creating an Amazon Machine Image, and an EBS snapshot and by configuring an Elastic IP address. Finally, you will practice recovering from instance, volume and availability zone failures.

Before you start, here are some key things to keep in mind:

**Selecting an availability zone**
You will specify a zone when launching an instance or when creating an EBS volume. Remember that an EBS volume can only be attached to an instance, if the instance and the volume are both in the same zone.

**File system on EBS**
The EBS volume is a raw block storage device. To make it usable, you will need to install a file system on it, and then you will need to mount it. Remember to configure the fstab so the volume mounts automatically when the server restarts.

**MySQL's data directory**
MySQL normally uses /var/lib/mysql as the data directory, this directory in the root volume. You will need to configure this data directory to point to the new data volume that you will create.

**Elastic IP vs. Public IP address**

When you associate the Elastic IP address to an instance, the instance's public IP address will be lost. Remember to use the Elastic IP address to access the instance via HTTP or via SSH.

## Amazon Machine Image

You will create an Amazon Machine Image in this chapter. Remember that this image is different from the one you created in the previous chapter, this one will have the app, the MySQL server, and data volume related configurations. Don't delete the image from chapter 1, you will need it later. You can delete the image created here, once you finish this chapter.

## Amazon Machine Image and the data volume

When creating the Amazon Machine Image, remember not to include the data volume in the image. The image should include just the root volume, the root volume has our app and configurations. You will use the EBS snapshot to restore data.

## EBS snapshot and the data volume

Remember to create the EBS snapshot of just the data volume, not the root volume. The root volume is already backed up in the Amazon Machine Image.

## A. SET UP APP WITH LOCAL DATABASE

1. Launch an EC2 instance as follows:

---

**Amazon Machine Image**
Use the image created in chapter 1.

**Instance type**
t2.micro

**VPC**

---

Use the default VPC again.

**Security Group**
Use the default security group.

**Other Configurations**
Use default values.

2. Install MySQL server.

# SSH into the server and run this command below. You will need to enter a password, twice. Remember this password, you will use it in the app later
sudo apt-get install mysql-server

3. Test the MySQL server installation.

# run this mysql command with the 'root' user, -p is for password
mysql -u root -p
<Enter password when prompted>

# exit mysql, to get back to Ubuntu
mysql> exit

4. Configure the MySQL connection details in the app.

# edit localdb.php page, specify mysql server's user and password, user should be root and password will be what you configured during mysql installation
sudo vi /var/www/html/localdb.php

```
// Configure local db connection details in this line in the
PHP page
$con=mysqli_connect('localhost','DB_USERNAME','DB_PAS
SWORD');
```

5. Verify the Local Db page, visit
http://EC2_INSTANCE_PUBLIC_IP/localdb.php. You should see
a 'connected' message.

**B. PREPARE FOR FAILURES**

**CONFIGURE A DATA VOLUME**
1. Create a new EBS volume as follows:

**Volume size**
Set to 1 GB, the minimum size.

**Availability Zone**
Set to the EC2 instance's zone.

**Other Configurations**
Use default values.

2. Attach the data volume to the instance.

**Device Name**
Leave at the default value: /dev/sdf

3. Install a file system on the data volume.

```
# SSH into the instance before you run these commands
# Check if data volume exists, device with name xvdf
should exist
```

```
lsblk

# Install file system on data volume
sudo mkfs -t ext4 /dev/xvdf
```

4. Mount the volume.

```
# Create a mount point, a folder to which the volume will
be mounted
sudo mkdir /data

# Mount the volume to the mount point
sudo mount /dev/xvdf /data
```

5. Configure fstab to ensure the data volume will be mounted upon a restart.

```
# Backup /etc/fstab file
sudo cp /etc/fstab /etc/fstab_bkp

# Open /etc/fstab to edit it
sudo vi /etc/fstab

# Copy the whole line below and paste to bottom of fstab
file, and save
/dev/xvdf /data    ext4   defaults,nofail 0    2

# Test for mount errors
sudo mount -a
```

**CONFIGURE MYSQL TO USE DATA VOLUME**
1. Stop MySQL server.

```
sudo systemctl stop mysql
```

2. Copy contents of MySQL's data directory to /data, the mount point of your data volume.

```
sudo rsync -av /var/lib/mysql /data
```

3. Edit the MySQL configuration to change the server's data directory to point to the new mount point.

```
# backup the mysql.conf file
sudo cp /etc/mysql/mysql.conf.d/mysqld.cnf
/etc/mysql/mysql.conf.d/mysqld.cnf_bkp

# open the mysql.conf file to edit
sudo vi /etc/mysql/mysql.conf.d/mysqld.cnf

# change datadir to this and save the file
datadir=/data/mysql
```

4. Edit the AppArmor alias configuration to point to the new data directory.

```
# open apparmor alias file to edit
sudo vi /etc/apparmor.d/tunables/alias

# add this line at the bottom of the file and save
alias /var/lib/mysql/ -> /data/mysql/,
```

5. Restart Apparmor.

```
sudo systemctl restart apparmor
```

6. Restart Mysql.

```
sudo mkdir /var/lib/mysql/mysql -p # this is to pass env
checks
sudo systemctl start mysql
```

## CONFIGURE ELASTIC IP ADDRESS
1. Allocate an Elastic IP address.
2. Associate the Elastic IP address to your EC2 instance.
3. Verify the localdb app page using the Elastic IP address in the browser, like this: http://ELASTIC_IP/localdb.php. You should see a 'connected' message.

## CREATE AN AMAZON MACHINE IMAGE

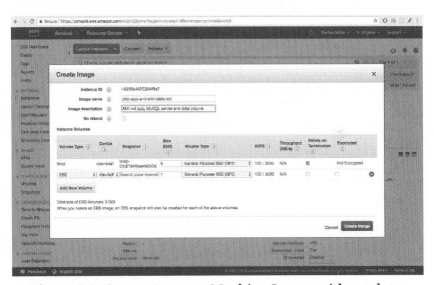

Figure 2.2: Create Amazon Machine Image without data volume

1. Create an image of your EC2 instance as follows:

30

> **Instance volumes**
> Select only the root volume, remove the data volume.
>
> **Other Configurations**
> Use default values.

## CREATE EBS SNAPSHOT

1. Create an EBS snapshot of the data volume (not of the root volume).

## C. PRACTICE RECOVERING FROM FAILURES

### RECOVER FROM INSTANCE FAILURE

1. Assume your instance has failed.
2. Stop the failed instance.
3. Detach the data volume.
4. Disassociate the Elastic IP address.
5. Delete the failed instance (just to avoid mixing up instances in the next set of steps).
6. Launch a replacement server in the same availability zone (the zone that has the failed instance).
7. Attach the data volume to the replacement server.
8. Associate the Elastic IP address with the replacement server.
9. Restart the replacement server.
10. Verify the localdb.php page from your browser - http://ELASTIC_IP/localdb.php. You should see a 'connected' message.

### RECOVER FROM DATA VOLUME FAILURE

1. Assume the data volume has failed.
2. Stop the instance.
3. Detach the failed volume.

4. Delete the failed volume (just to avoid mixing up volumes in the next set of steps).
5. Use the EBS snapshot to create a new EBS volume. Ensure the new volume is in the same availability zone (the one that has the failed volume).
6. Attach the new EBS volume to the instance. Use the default device name - /dev/sdf.
7. Start the EC2 instance.
8. Verify the localdb.php page from your browser - http://ELASTIC_IP/localdb.php. You should see a 'connected' message.

## RECOVER FROM AVAILABILITY ZONE FAILURE

1. Assume your zone has failed.
2. Dissociate the Elastic IP from the instance in the failed zone.
3. Delete the instance and its data volume (just to avoid mixing up instances and volumes in the next set of steps).
4. Use the Amazon Machine Image to launch a replacement instance in a different zone.
5. Use the EBS snapshot to restore data into a new EBS volume, in the same availability zone as in the step above.
6. Attach the EBS volume to the replacement server.
7. Associate the Elastic IP address with the replacement server.
8. Restart the replacement server.
9. Verify the localdb.php page from your browser - http://ELASTIC_IP/localdb.php. You should see a 'connected' message.

# CHAPTER 3: FAULT TOLERANCE

## Introduction

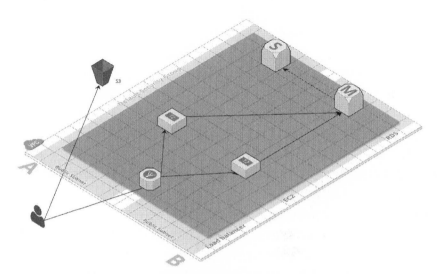

Figure 3.1: Fault tolerant multi-tier architecture

**Objectives**
To implement a fault tolerant, multi-tier architecture. To eliminate downtime and data loss, the limitations of the single instance architecture you saw in the previous chapter.

**Key steps**
Launch EC2 instances in multiple availability zones, create an application load balancer, separate database into its own tier, centralize images, configure and verify the app.

**You will learn about**
RDS, S3, Application Load Balancer, Sticky Sessions, RDS Multi-AZ deployment option, AWS Availability Zones. Best practices of using multiple instances and multiple zones,

centralizing content and database, and that of using database replication.

## Discussion

To avoid downtime, you will need multiple instances. If an instance fails, other instances will take up the slack, and the application will stay up. You should distribute these instances in multiple availability zones as well. Availability zones are designed to be independent, if a zone fails, say due to power failure or due to loss of Internet connectivity, other zones remain unaffected because each zone has its own set of power supplies and Internet connections.

You will use an application load balancer to distribute requests to the EC2 instances. Your domain should point to the load balancer (note: you will not need to do this in this project) so that user requests go to the load balancer, the load balancer, in turn, will forward the requests to the EC2 instances using algorithms such as round robin routing.

You will need to move the database to another tier. If each of your instances had a local database server, you would need a way to synchronize the data in each of these database servers. That is not possible, relational databases are designed to have a single master. For the same reason, you will need to centralize images and centralize sessions as well. It is hard to synchronize the content and the sessions that will be created or updated in each instance.

You will set up your database in RDS. RDS is a databases platform, it makes database administration simple by automating routine administration activities such as software installation, software upgrades, and database backups.

The RDS multi-AZ deployment option automatically creates a standby server and replicates data into it from the primary instance using a master-slave configuration. The standby server is always in a different availability zone. If the primary RDS instance fails, or if the primary instance's availability zone fails, RDS will automatically failover to the standby instance.

Note that the RDS multi-AZ option also eliminates data loss. If the volume on the primary instance fails, the data is safe in the standby instance. The data in the standby is always up-to-date because the replication from the primary to the secondary is synchronous.

You will centralize images in S3. S3 is a scalable, durable and highly available storage service. In general, S3 is cheaper than EBS as well. It is simple to use, each of your images in S3 will have a URL, the app will send this URL to your app user, and the user's browser will use the URL to fetch the image directly from S3.

You will centralize sessions in a separate database in the next chapter. In this chapter, you will use the load balancers Sticky Sessions feature. When this feature is enabled the load balancer uses a browser cookie to track a particular user and sends that users requests to the same instance, the instance on which this user will create a session. A centralized sessions database is better, but it is more difficult to set up, you don't have to change the application to use sticky sessions.

## Implementation

You will now launch two app servers in two zones, and create an application load balancer in front of these instances. You will configure Sticky Sessions in the load balancer. You will centralize images in S3 and also separate the MySQL database into its own tier, using a Multi-AZ RDS instance.

Before you start, here are some key points to remember:

**RDS configuration**
Use the default VPC, and the t2.micro instance type for RDS instances as well.

**RDS security group**
To avoid connectivity problems between the EC2 instance and the RDS instance, remember to use the default security group for your RDS instance as well. The default security group is configured to allow connectivity on all ports if both servers, the EC2 instance, and the RDS instance, use the same security group.

**S3 bucket names**
S3 bucket names are unique across all AWS customers, much like domain names. If your bucket name is already taken by someone else, try another name.

**Verifying session stickiness**
To help verify session stickiness, you will include a server identifier, say the public IP address of the instance, in the session page in that instance. This way, you will be able to identify which server your request has been forwarded to by the load balancer.

**LAUNCH TWO INSTANCE IN TWO AVAILABILITY ZONES**
1. Launch an EC2 instance as follows:

| **Amazon Machine Image** |
| Use the image created in chapter 1. |

**Availability Zone**
Select any zone, say 1a.

**VPC**
Use the default VPC.

**Security Group**
Select the default security group.

**Other Configurations**
Use default values.

2. Launch a second EC2 instance as follows:

**Availability Zone**
Select a different zone, say 1b.

**Other configurations**
Same as configured for the first instance.

**CREATE THE APPLICATION LOAD BALANCER**
1. Create an application load balancer as follows:

**Type**
Application load balancer.

**VPC**
Use default VPC.

**Availability Zones**
Use the same two zones used by your EC2 instances.

**Security Group**
Use the default security group.

**Target Group**
Create a new target group.

**Other Configurations**
Use default values.

2. Register the two EC2 instances with the load balancer's target group.
3. Wait for the load balancer state to change to 'active'.
4. Wait for instances in the target group to change to the 'healthy' status.
5. Use the load balancer DNS name in your browser to test the app, like this - http://ELB_DNS_NAME/index.php.

**CONFIGURE STICKY SESSIONS**

Figure 3.2: Testing sticky sessions

1. Edit the session.php page in the first instance and add the instance's public IP address to the h1 tag.

```
# SSH into the instance using its public IP address
# Open the session.php page to edit it
```

```
sudo vi /var/www/html/session.php

# Add the instance public IP address to the h1 tag like this
and save the file
<h1>Session - 54.227.65.162</h1>
```

2. In a similar manner, edit the session.php in the second instance and add the second instance's public IP address to the h1 tag.
3. Test the application via the load balancer and verify that the load balancer does a round robin distribution. Each time you refresh the session.php page, your request should be sent to the other server, and you should see a different IP address.
4. Enable sticky sessions from the target group settings as follows:

**Session stickiness**
Set to 'enabled.

**Stickiness duration**
Set to 1 day.

5. Verify that the session is now sticky. Each time you refresh, the load balancer should keep sending your requests to a single instance. Create a session by submitting the form, verify that you see a 'welcome' message each time you refresh.

**SEPARATE DB TIER USING RDS**

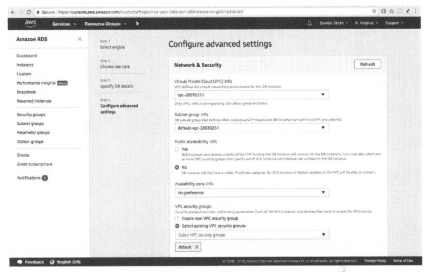

Figure 3.3: RDS networking configuration

1. Launch an RDS instance as follows:

**DB engine**
Select MySQL.

**Instance type**
Choose t2.micro.

**Multi-AZ deployment**
Say 'Yes'.

**VPC**
Select the default VPC.

**Security Group**
Use the default security group.

**Other Configurations**
Use default values.

2. Note down the RDS master username and password you configure, you will use these in the PHP app in subsequent steps.

3. Wait for the instance to become 'available' and for the RDS endpoint to become available as well.

4. Test connectivity from an EC2 instance.

```
# SSH into an instance and run this command:
mysql -h <RDS_end_point> -u <RDS_master_user> -p

# Exit Mysql connection and back to Ubuntu
mysql> exit
```

**CENTRALIZE IMAGES IN S3**

Figure 3.4: Access image in S3 using images' URL

1. Create an S3 bucket.
2. Upload an image, any image will do.
3. Click on the uploaded image, make the image 'public'.
4. Use the object URL of the uploaded image in your browser and test if you can view the image.

**CONFIGURE & VERIFY APPLICATION**
1. SSH into the first EC2 instance.

2. Configure the RDS hostname, the RDS master user and the RDS master user's password in the rds.php page:

```
# open rds.php to edit it
sudo vi /var/www/html/rds.php

# configure RDS host, user and password in this line, and
save the file
$con=mysqli_connect('RDS_HOSTNAME', 'DB_USERNAME',
'DB_PASSWORD');
```

3. Verify the RDS page from your browser - http://EC2_INSTANCE_PUBLIC_IP/rds.php, you should see a 'connected' message.
4. Configure the URL of the image in S3 in the s3_image.php page:

```
# open s3_image.php to edit it
sudo vi /var/www/html/s3_image.php

# configure the full URL of the S3 image, including https://
in this line, and save the file
<img src="S3_IMAGE_URL" />
```

5. Verify the S3 image page from your browser - http://EC2_INSTANCE_PUBLIC_IP/s3_image.php, you should see the S3 image displayed.
6. Repeat the steps above for the second EC2 instance.
7. Verify the RDS and S3 image pages via the load balancer DNS name as well.

# CHAPTER 4: SCALABILITY IN APP LAYER

## Introduction

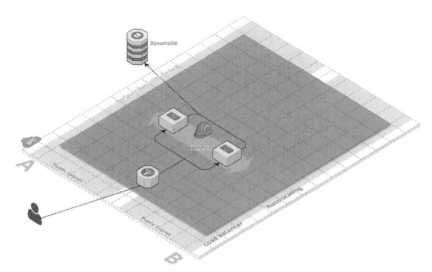

Figure 4.1: Scalability in app layer

**Objectives**

To implement scalability in the app layer. The goal is to be able to easily add capacity when load increases so that the app performs well at elevated loads. For cost-efficiency purposes, you need to be able to, just as easily, remove capacity when the load decreases. To centralize sessions in a database outside the EC2 instances, so that sessions are not lost when servers are removed.

**Key steps**

Centralize sessions in DynamoDB, Create IAM role to allow the app to access DynamoDB, set up an auto-scaling group behind a load balancer.

**You will learn about**

Auto-scaling groups, DynamoDB, IAM roles, AWS managed IAM policies, Customer managed IAM policies. Best practice of centralizing sessions, and of setting up permissions using principles of least privileges.

## Discussion

In the real world, the load on a system changes over time. Business apps tend to be used more during business hours, online retail sites see massive increases in transaction volumes during the Thanksgiving holiday and banks need more servers for month-end batch programs.

Traditionally, companies provisioned capacity for peak loads. However, this is not cost-efficient because the overall utilization of the infrastructure is low. In AWS, you can closely match demand and capacity, and achieve high performance and cost efficiency at the same time.

EC2 auto-scaling groups are used to scale out (increase the number of servers) and scale in (decrease the number of servers) easily. The group can be scaled manually, using scheduled policies (add more servers at 9 AM every day) or using auto-scaling policies (add servers if CPU of the group goes above 80%).

When the auto-scaling group scales in, some servers are terminated. Sessions created on those servers are lost and users will need to create sessions again. If this happens frequently, the user experience can become unacceptably poor. You will, therefore, need to centralize sessions, just like you centralized the database in RDS and the images in S3 in the previous chapter.

DynamoDB is a good service for managing sessions. This is AWS's NoSQL offering. It is a server-less technology, you don't have to provision servers, install and upgrade software or worry about fault tolerance and scalability, all of this is built-in.

DynamoDB has a proprietary interface and an app needs to use the AWS SDK to talk to it. Access to DynamoDB is controlled using IAM, another AWS service. You will need to attach an IAM role to your EC2 instances, the role will have permissions to access the sessions table in DynamoDB. The app running on such an EC2 instance will be able to assume the IAM role to gain access to the DynamoDB table.

# Implementation

You will now create a sessions table in DynamoDB and configure an IAM role that will allow your app to talk to DynamoDB. You will then set up an auto-scaling group with a load balancer in front of it. You will verify that the app is able to use DynamoDB to manage sessions.

Before you start, here are some key points to note:

**DynamoDB table**
You must create a table in the North Virginia (US-EAST-1) region with name 'sessions' and primary key 'id'. These are hard-coded in the dyn_session.php page.

**IAM role**
Test the DynamoDB sessions page and the IAM role from a single EC2 instance first, this will make troubleshooting simpler. After you get it to work with a single instance, configure the IAM role in your auto-scaling launch configuration.

## IAM custom policy

The IAM custom policy restricts app access to a few actions - PutItem, GetItem and UpdateItem and restricts access only to the sessions table in the US-EAST-1 region. In the steps below, for easier troubleshooting, you will start with a simpler FullDynamoDBAccess policy, once the setup works with this policy, you will configure the custom policy.

## Attaching the IAM role

Don't forget to attach the IAM role to the EC2 instance and to the auto-scaling Launch Configuration. The DynamoDB sessions page will not work without the IAM role.

## Troubleshooting

Tail the Apache web server's error log file for diagnostic information.

```
tail -f /var/log/apache2/error.log
```

## CREATE SESSIONS TABLES IN DYNAMODB

1. Create a table 'sessions' with primary key 'id'. You must use the North Virginia (US-EAST-1) region.

## CONFIGURE IAM ROLE

Figure 4.2: Attach IAM role to an EC2 instance

1. Create an IAM role with an AWS managed policy - DynamoDBFullAccess.
2. Launch an EC2 instance in the usual manner and then attach this IAM role to it. Select the instance and from 'Instance actions', 'Instance settings', 'Attach/Replace IAM role'.
3. Verify the DynamoDB sessions page from your browser - http://EC2_INSTANCE_PUBLIC_IP/dyn_session.php. You should be able to create a session and when you refresh you should continue to see the 'welcome' message.
4. Create a custom IAM policy, use this JSON document:

```
{
   "Version": "2012-10-17",
   "Statement": [
      {
         "Sid": "VisualEditor0",
         "Effect": "Allow",
         "Action": [
```

```
        "dynamodb:PutItem",
        "dynamodb:GetItem",
        "dynamodb:UpdateItem"
      ],
      "Resource":
"arn:aws:dynamodb:us-east-1:*:table/sessions"
    }
  ]
}
```

5. Remove the AWS managed policy attached to the IAM role and replace it with the custom policy.
6. Verify the DynamoDB sessions page once again.

## SET UP AUTO-SCALING GROUP

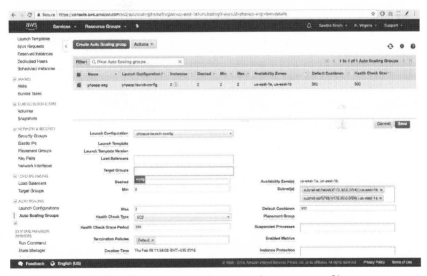

Figure 4.3: Configure target group in auto-scaling group

1. Create an application load balancer as follows:

VPC

Use the default VPC.

**Availability Zones**
Select two zones, say 1a and 1b.

**Security Group**
Use the default security group.

**Other Configurations**
Use default values.

2. Create an auto-scaling group launch configuration as follows:

**Amazon Machine Image**
Use the image created in chapter 1.

**Instance Type**
t2.micro

**Security Group**
Default security group.

**IAM role**
Attach the IAM role created earlier in this chapter.

**Other Configurations**
Use default values.

3. Create an auto-scaling group as follows:

**Launch configuration**
Use the launch configuration created in the previous step.

**VPC**
Use the default VPC.

**Availability Zones**
Use the same two zones that you configured for your load balancer.

**Capacity**
Set to 2.

**Other Configurations**
Use default values.

4. Configure load balancer's target group in the auto-scaling group.
5. Verify the DynamoDB sessions page using the load balancer's DNS endpoint.
6. Verify the DynamoDB table as well, the item's expiry timestamp should be updated every time you refresh the DynamoDB sessions page.

Figure 4.4: Session item in DynamoDB table

# CHAPTER 5: SCALABILITY IN DATA LAYERS

## Introduction

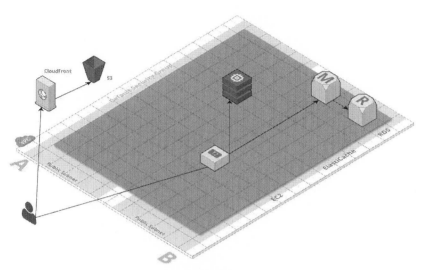

Figure 5.1: Scalability in data layers

**Objectives**
To address scalability for the data layers of the app. The data layers include the database in RDS, and the content in S3.

**Key steps**
Create an RDS read replica instance, create a Memcached cluster, set up a CloudFront distribution in front of S3, configure these elements and verify the app.

**You will learn about**
RDS, ElastiCache, CloudFront, Memcached clusters, and RDS Read Replicas.

# Discussion

Relational databases are hard to scale horizontally (more servers) because it is hard to collate data from multiple servers quickly, especially when using SQL joins. So traditionally, these have been scaled vertically (bigger servers). AWS offers servers with dozens of vCPUs and hundreds of GBs of RAM, so scaling RDS instances vertically is easy enough.

Another way of scaling the database is to offload requests to database read replicas or to in-memory cache databases. This reduces the load on the primary database and makes the overall system more scalable. The database read replicas and cache servers can themselves be scaled vertically, and horizontally. Offloading of requests away from the primary database can also lead to cost savings because you may end up using less capacity overall.

S3, your image store is already highly scalable. You can store any number of objects in S3 and users can make any number of requests to it. S3 is not scalable on its own from a network perspective though. If your app has users around the world, users far away from the AWS region housing your S3 content will not see the same network performance as users close to your AWS region. This is due to network latency.

CloudFront is AWS's Content Distribution Network. It consists of a network of edge locations that house cache servers, the edge locations are located in major cities around the world. CloudFront is configured in front of S3, and app users fetch content from CloudFront instead of from S3. Cached content is served to a user from an edge location closest to the user, thus minimizing the effects of network latency.

Offloading content requests to CloudFront may lead to lower network costs as well, CloudFront network costs are lower compared to S3 network costs, and there is no cost to data transfer from S3 to CloudFront.

## Implementation

You will create an RDS read replica, a Memcached cluster, and a CloudFront distribution. You will then configure these in the PHP app and verify the respective app pages. Here are a few key points to note before you get started:

**RDS Replica user and password**
The RDS read replica is a separate instance and has a separate endpoint, but it has the same master user and password as the primary RDS instance. Use the RDS master user and password when connecting to the replica.

**RDS Replica region**
Create the replica in the same region. In this project, you want to use the replica as a scalability solution and you want the network latency between the EC2 instances and the replica to be as low as possible.

**ElastiCache default node type**
The default node type in ElastiCache is r3.large, this is not free tier eligible. Don't forget to choose t2.micro when creating the cluster.

**ElastiCache security group**
Make sure you select the default VPC and the default security group when creating the cluster. These are configured for easy connectivity from the EC2 instance.

## CloudFront distribution

It can take up to 20 minutes for the CloudFront distribution to be deployed. The S3 image may not accessible via CloudFront until the distribution is fully deployed.

### LAUNCH EC2 INSTANCE

1. Launch an EC2 instance using the Amazon Machine Image from chapter 1 in the usual manner.

### CREATE RDS READ REPLICA

1. Launch an RDS instance in the usual manner.
2. Create a read replica of the RDS instance as follows:

---

**Region**
Use the same region as the primary instance's region.

**Instance type**
Use t2.micro as always.

**Other Configurations**
Use default values.

---

3. Wait for the replica instance to become available, and for the replica's endpoint to become available.
4. Verify connectivity to the read replica from the EC2 instance.

---

```
# connect to the replica using this command
# use the replica's endpoint, but the primary instance's
user and password
mysql -h <RDS_READ_REPLICA_ENDPOINT> -u
<RDS_MASTER_USER> -p

# exit mysql connection and back to Ubuntu
```

```
mysql > exit
```

## CREATE ELASTICACHE (MEMCACHED) CLUSTER

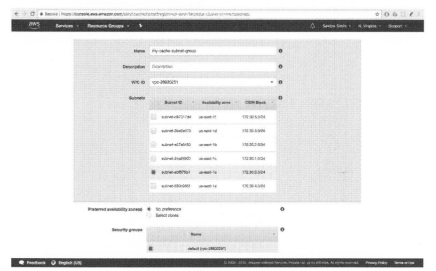

Figure 5.2: Configure a DB subnet group in ElastiCache

1. Create a Memcached cluster in ElastiCache as follows:

**Instance type**
Change to t2.micro.

**Number of nodes**
Set to 1.

**Subnet Group**
Create a new subnet group. Choose the default VPC and
select one or more subnets.

**Security Groups**
Use the default security group.

> **Other Configurations**
> Use default values.

2. Wait for the cache cluster and its endpoint to become available.
3. Use Telnet to verify connectivity from the EC2 instance.

```
# SSH into the EC2 instance and telnet to the cluster
telnet <CLUSTER_END_POINT> 11211

# try the get command, you will receive nothing because
nothing is set as yet in the cache
get a

# to exit the telnet session and go back to Ubuntu
quit
```

**Set up CloudFront distribution**

Figure 5.3: Access S3 image using a CloudFront URL

1. Create an S3 bucket with a 'public' image, unless you have the bucket already.
2. Create a CloudFront web distribution as follows:

3. Use the CloudFront distributions DNS endpoint to verify access to the image, like this - https://<CLOUDFRONT_DNS>/<YOUR_S3_IMG_NAME>. You should see the S3 image displayed.

**CONFIGURE & VERIFY APP**
1. Edit rds_rr.php and configure the RDS read replica details as follows:

RDS_RR_HOST_NAME
Configure the RDS read replica's endpoint.

RDS_USERNAME
Set to the primary RDS instance's master username.

RDS_PASSWORD
Set to the primary RDS instance's master user's password.

2. Verify the rds_rr.php page in your browser, you should see the 'connected' message
3. Edit the memcached.php page as follows:

MEMCACHED_ENDPOINT
Configure the Memcached cluster's endpoint.

4. Verify the memcached.php page in the browser, you should see a 'connected' message.
5. Edit cf_image.php as follows:

---

CLOUDFRONT_URL
Configure the CloudFront URL for the image.

---

6. Verify the cf_image.php in your browser, the page should display the image that is stored in S3.

# CHAPTER 6: PRIVATE CONTENT

## Introduction

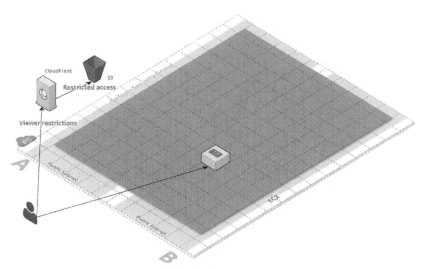

Figure 6.1: Private Content

**Objectives**
To restrict access to the content that is stored in S3, only
authorized users should be able to view the content.

**Key steps**
Remove 'public' access to content in S3, allow CloudFront to
access S3 content, configure CloudFront to deliver content
only in response to valid signed URLs.

**You will learn about**
S3 access control lists, S3 bucket policies, CloudFront Origin
Access Identity, CloudFront signed URLs, and CloudFront key
pairs.

# Discussion

In a single instance architecture, an app can easily control access to content such as images or video. This is because the content is served from the server. When a user requests the image page, the server verifies that the user is authorized, and sends back the image stored in the file system.

In the current architecture, the image in S3 is served by CloudFront, not by the server. The app sends the URL of the image to the user, and the user's browser uses the URL to fetch the image directly from CloudFront.

To control access to content served by CloudFront, you need a way for the app to tell CloudFront whether or not a request is authorized. Your app will do this using signed URLs. The URLs you have used so far in this project are static, a signed URL is dynamic. A new URL is generated every time a user visits the image page, each URL is valid for a short time, after that it expires. CloudFront will serve the content only if the URL has not expired.

The app signs the URLs using a private key. You can create a CloudFront key pair in the AWS management console. This is how CloudFront knows that the signed URL is generated by a trusted app. It uses the public key of the key pair to validate the URL's signature.

Signed URLs prevent unauthorized users from accessing content via CloudFront. You also need to ensure that unauthorized users cannot access content directly from S3. You will need to edit the S3 object permissions and block public access to it. However this will prevent CloudFront from accessing images in S3, to remedy this, you will create an S3 bucket policy that will allow only CloudFront to access the bucket's content.

## Implementation

You will restrict access to the S3 image by removing 'public' access. You will configure CloudFront to create an S3 bucket policy that will allow CloudFront to access the content in S3. You will then configure CloudFront to restrict viewer access, in other words, users will need signed URLs to access content. Finally, you will configure the app with a CloudFront private key, so that app can generate signed URLs.

Before you start, here are some useful tips :

**Restrict bucket access**
This phrase used in the CloudFront configuration pages can be confusing because what you will do here is 'allow' CloudFront access to the S3 bucket. When you configure this, CloudFront will create a bucket policy in S3 that will allow CloudFront's Origin Access Identity to read the contents of the S3 bucket. The policy allows only CloudFront to access the bucket, hence the name 'restrict bucket access'.

**Private key**
You will install a CloudFront private key on the EC2 instance. The PHP app will use this private key to generate signed URLs. When copying this key on to the server, you must copy and paste the entire private key including the first and the last lines -----BEGIN RSA PRIVATE KEY----- and -----END RSA PRIVATE KEY-----.

**RESTRICT S3 ACCESS**

1. Remove 'public access' on the image in your S3 bucket. You can do this from the objects permissions tab, for the group 'Everyone', remove 'Read Object' access.
2. Test the URL of the image in your browser. Verify that the image is no longer available, you should see a 'permissions denied' message.

**RESTRICT BUCKET ACCESS TO CLOUDFRONT**

Figure 6.2: Restrict bucket access to CloudFront

1. Edit Origin settings of your CloudFront distribution as follows:

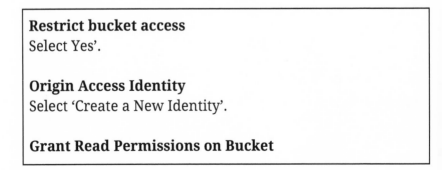

**Restrict bucket access**
Select Yes'.

**Origin Access Identity**
Select 'Create a New Identity'.

**Grant Read Permissions on Bucket**

Set to 'Yes, Update Bucket Policy'. This will update the S3 bucket policy to allow the distribution's Origin Access Identity read access to the contents of the bucket.

2. Wait for these configuration changes to be deployed, this may take up to 20 minutes.
3. Visit the CloudFront URL of the image from your browser. Verify that you can view the image via CloudFront.

## RESTRICT VIEWER ACCESS

Figure 6.3: Restrict viewer access

1. Edit the Behavior settings of your CloudFront distribution as follows:

**Restrict viewer access**
Select 'Yes'.

**Trusted Signers**
Set to 'Self'.

2. Wait for these configuration changes to be deployed, this may take up to 20 minutes.
3. Visit the CloudFront URL of the image from your browser. Verify that you cannot view the image via CloudFront. You should see a 'Missing Key' error. This means CloudFront will now serve images only when signed URLs are used.

**CREATE CLOUDFRONT KEY PAIR**

1. Create a CloudFront key pair. Visit your 'AWS account settings', then 'My Security Credentials', and the 'CloudFront Key Pairs' section. Ensure you download the private key to your computer and note the Access Key Id, you will use these in the app.

**CONFIGURE & VERIFY APP**

← C ① 54.165.244.248/signedurl_image.php  ☆ 0 ⚙ ✎

**Signed CloudFront Image**

Figure 6.4: App page with image accessed using a signed URL

1. Launch an EC2 instance and SSH into it.
2. Install the private key on the EC2 instance as follows:

---

**Private key file's path and name**
Create a file 'cf-private-key.pem' in the home folder: /home/ubuntu.

**Contents of the file**

---

> Copy the contents of the private key file on your computer and paste into this file and then save the file.

3. Configure the CloudFront signed URL PHP page.

```
# open the signedurl_image.php page for editing
sudo vi /var/www/html/signedurl_image.php

# configure the full cloudfront url of the image including
https:// in this line
'url'        => 'FULL_URL_OF_IMAGE_VIA_CLOUDFRONT',

# configure the path to the private key on the server in this
line
# this should be /home/ubuntu/cf_private-key.pem
'private_key' =>
'PATH_TO_PRIVATE_KEY_FILE_ON_EC2_SERVER',

# configure the key pair id in this line
'key_pair_id' => 'KEY_PAIR_ID'
```

4. Verify the signedurl_image.php page in your browser, you should see the image displayed on your screen.
5. Verify the cloudfront_image.php and s3_image.php pages as well, these pages should NOT display the image.

# CHAPTER 7: EASE OF DEPLOYMENT

## Introduction

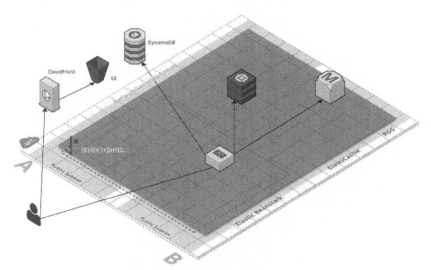

Figure 7.1: Ease of Deployment

**Objectives**
To incorporate ease of deployment in the architecture so you can deploy app updates frequently.

**Key steps**
Create an Elastic Beanstalk environment, deploy one by one, the different versions of the app - the hello world version, multi-tier version, scalable version, signed URL version.

**You will learn about**
Elastic Beanstalk, Beanstalk environment variables, and IAM customer managed policies.

# Discussion

How would you deploy app updates to an auto-scaled environment with dozens of servers? For every app update, you could deploy the update on a standalone instance, create a new Amazon Machine Image from there, then create a new launch configuration and a new auto-scaling group to replace the one you have.

As things stand, environment configurations such as the RDS instance endpoint are hard-coded in the app, so you cannot reuse the same Amazon Machine Images and launch configurations in your dev, test or live environments, you would need to duplicate the process for each environment you manage. This type of process works fine if updates are infrequent, but can be unwieldy in modern agile projects.

AWS offers multiple deployment and provisioning type of services - OpsWorks, CodeDeploy, CloudFormation and Elastic Beanstalk, each service has its pros and cons. Elastic Beanstalk is the easiest way to manage web app environments. You simply upload your code and the service does the rest, you don't need to manage Amazon Machine Images, don't need to do configuration management, you don't even need to SSH into a server.

A Beanstalk environment can be a single instance or a load balanced and auto-scaled one. Beanstalk environment variables can be used to manage environment configurations such as the RDS instance endpoint, these don't need to be hard-coded in the app anymore. The same app will work on any dev, test or live environment. An app update can be deployed usually with a single click or via a single command in the Beanstalk CLI.

# Implementation

You will now create a Beanstalk environment and deploy multiple versions of the project app. First, you will deploy the hello world version, this has just the index page. Next, the multi-tier version, this version has the RDS, S3, and session pages. Next, the scalable version, this has the DynamoDB sessions, the RDS read replica, and the Memcached pages. And finally, you will deploy the signed URL version, which has the CloudFront signed URL page.

Here are some key points to keep in mind before you start:

**Clone on the local computer**
You will clone the app on a local computer. You will use this clone to create archives of different versions of the app for upload to the Beanstalk environment.

**This app is different**
You will use a different git repository this time. This repository has a modified version of the app, this app uses environment variables, for app configurations such as the RDS endpoint, instead of hard-coded values.

**Environment variables**
You will configure environment variables using the Beanstalk management console. This way, in a real project, you can use the same app for multiple dev, test or live environments.

**RDS and Beanstalk**
When creating the Beanstalk environment, you will see an option to use RDS, don't select this option. If you did, a new RDS instance will be created as part of the Beanstalk

environment, you don't want this, you will use an external (external to the Beanstalk environment) RDS instance.

## Configure IAM role

When you deploy the scalable version of the app, you will replace the default Beanstalk IAM role with your own IAM role, the one that allows your app to access the sessions table in DynamoDB. Your app on Beanstalk will now be able to talk to DynamoDB. However, when you replace the default role, Beanstalk will lose permissions to manage AWS resources on your behalf. So you will first attach a policy - AWSElasticBeanstalkWebTier - to your IAM role and then attach the role to the environment.

## CLONE BEANSTALK VERSION OF APP

1. Clone the app on a local computer:

```
# note that this is a different repository to the one you
used in chapter 1
git clone
https://savitras@bitbucket.org/savitras/aws-course-php-ap
p-beanstalk.git
```

2. Inspect the app, this app uses environment variables instead of hard-coded configurations:

```
# change into folder
cd aws-course-php-app-beanstalk/

# inspect contents of app folder
ls

# inspect PHP pages
cat rds.php
```

```
# check git commits
git log --pretty=oneline
```

## DEPLOY HELLO WORLD VERSION

Figure 7.2: Hello world app in a Beanstalk environment

1. Create an archive of the hello world version of the app.

```
# check git commits
git log --pretty=oneline

# Checkout the hello world version of the app, use the
commit id of this version as shown below
git checkout
9d5bdd3ee2f73342bcd483deb0a1a6605704660a

# Use the git archive command to export the app into a zip
file:
git archive --format=zip HEAD >
aws-course-php-app-helloworld.zip
```

2. Create an Elastic Beanstalk environment as follows:

**Type**
Web Server Environment.

**Platform**
Select PHP.

**Environment Type**
Select single instance.

**Application Version**
Upload the app archive that you created in the previous step.

**Additional Resources**
DO NOT select 'Create an RDS DB instance with this environment'
DO select 'Create this environment inside a VPC'.

**Instance Type**
t2.micro

**VPC configuration**
Use the default VPC and select any subnet in this VPC.

**Security Group**
Use the default security group.

**Other Configurations**
Use default values.

3. Wait for the Beanstalk environment to become fully available.
4. Verify the app on the Beanstalk environment using the environment URL - http://BEANSTALK_ENV_URL, you should

see the 'hello world' message along with links to other app pages. The other pages won't work because this app version does not have these pages.

**DEPLOY MULTI-TIER VERSION**

Figure 7.3: Configure Beanstalk environment variables

1. Ensure you have an RDS instance and an S3 bucket (with a 'public' image) available.
2. Configure environment variables in the Beanstalk console. From 'Setup Configuration', find 'Software Configuration' and scroll down to find 'Environment properties'. Configure the following variables with appropriate values.

RDS_HOSTNAME

RDS_USERNAME

RDS_PASSWORD

S3_IMAGE_URL (use the full URL including http://)

3. Create an archive of the multi-tier version.

```
# Back to master
git checkout master

# check git commits
git log --pretty=oneline

# checkout multi-tier version of the app
git checkout
5ea9332a3df44446b6b9d96ed49e748a8d5b2f73

# Use the git archive command to export the app into a zip
file
git archive --format=zip HEAD >
aws-course-php-app-multi-tier.zip
```

4. Upload the archive to Beanstalk. Use the 'Upload' button under the 'Application versions'.
5. Select the uploaded version and use the 'Deploy' button to deploy this version on to the environment.
6. Verify the app using the environment URL, test the sessions, the S3 image, and the RDS pages.

**DEPLOY SCALABLE VERSION**

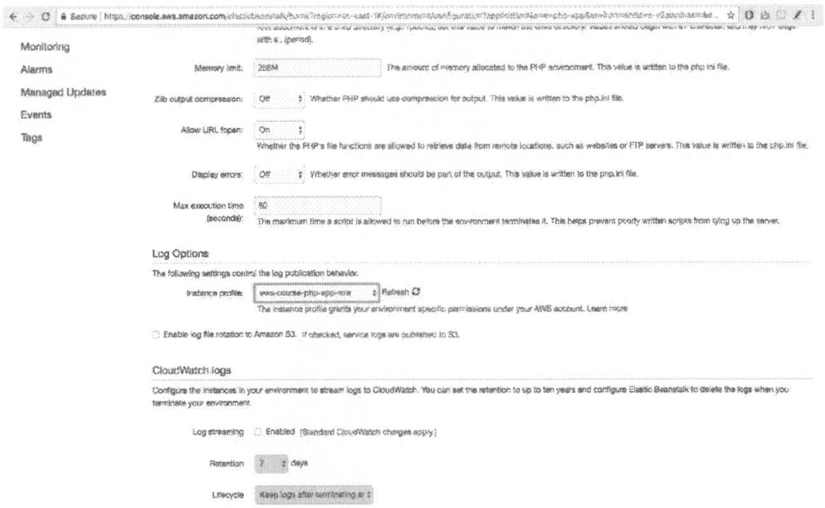

Figure 7.4: Configure IAM role in Beanstalk environment

1. Set up prerequisites for this version:
* A sessions table in DynamoDB.
* A Memcached cluster.
* An RDS instance with a read replica.
* An IAM role with access to the DynamoDB table.
2. To the IAM role attach this AWS managed policy -
AWSElasticBeanstalkWebTier.
3. Configure the Beanstalk environment as follows:

---

**Instance profile**
Select your IAM role

**Environment variables**
Configure following variables with appropriate values:

RDS_RR_HOSTNAME

MEMCACHED_ENDPOINT

---

DYN_REGION (set this to us-east-1)

CLOUDFRONT_IMAGE_URL (use the full URL including
https://)

4. Create an archive of the scalable version of the app.

```
# Back to master
git checkout master

# check git commits
git log --pretty=oneline

# checkout scalable version of the app
git checkout fa72343d5f1a31b4cec1c472307d13fc5393fb9c

# Use the git archive command to export the app into a zip
file
git archive --format=zip HEAD >
aws-course-php-app-scalable.zip
```

5. Upload the app archive.
6. Deploy the scalable version on to the environment.
7. Verify the app using the environment URL, test the
DynamoDB sessions page, the Memcached page, and the read
replica page.

**DEPLOY SECURE (SIGNED URL) VERSION**

Figure 7.5: Secure (Signed URL) app in Beanstalk

1. Create a CloudFront key pair, or reuse the key pair you created in chapter 6 - Private Content.
2. Create a new S3 bucket and upload the CloudFront private key file into it.
3. Update your IAM role with the custom policy provided below. This policy will allow the app to download the private key from the S3 bucket created above. Remember to add your S3 bucket's name to the policy.

```
{
    "Version": "2012-10-17",
    "Statement": [
        {
            "Sid": "VisualEditor0",
            "Effect": "Allow",
            "Action": "s3:GetObject",
            "Resource":
"arn:aws:s3:::<S3_BUCKET_WITH_PRIVATE_KEY>/*"
        }
    ]
}
```

4. Configure this environment variable in the Beanstalk environment with an appropriate value.

CLOUDFRONT_KEY_PAIR_ID

5. Create an archive of the secure version.

```
# Back to master
git checkout master

# checkout multi-tier version of the app
git checkout a48cf5de263ea7f89812c8e8f74d0f9703083422

# Edit the private key configuration file, add details of the
s3 location of your private key
vi .ebextensions/privatekey.config

# Add the name of the s3 bucket where you have stored
your private key below, e.g.
eb-pvtkey-us-east-1-123456789012
buckets: ["S3_BUCKET_WITH_PRIVATE_KEY"]

# Specify the URL of the private key file stored in your s3
bucket, e.g
https://s3.amazonaws.com/eb-pvtkey-us-east-1-1234567890
12/pk-APKAJ63NC4PRMDSDDWOI.pem
source: URL_OF_PRIVATE_KEY_IN_S3_BUCKET

# Commit the private key config
git add .ebextensions/privatekey.config
git commit

# Use the git archive command to export the app into a zip
file
git archive --format=zip HEAD >
aws-course-php-app-secure.zip
```

6. Upload and deploy the app archive.

7. Verify the app, test the signed URL page, you should see the image that is stored in S3 displayed on your screen.

# CHAPTER 8: NETWORK SECURITY

## Introduction

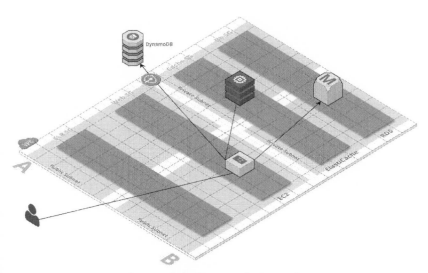

Figure 8.1: Network Security

**Objectives**
Thus far in this book, you have used the default VPC and the default security group. These are configured for easier connectivity, not for network security. In this chapter, you will implement strong network controls for your stack by creating a new VPC with public and private subnets and by configuring 'nested' security groups.

**Key steps**
Create a new VPC, create public and private subnets, setup nested security groups, create DB subnet groups, create a VPC service endpoint for DynamoDB, verify network setup.

**You will learn about**

VPCs, public and private subnets, VPC service endpoints, VPC service endpoint policies, and nested security groups.

# Discussion

A VPC is meant to be a private network, isolated from the Internet and isolated from other VPCs as well. The default VPC you have used thus far in this project is not really a private network, all its subnets are public and it auto-assigns a public IP address to any server launched inside it. This VPC is designed for easier connectivity, not for security, don't use it for any serious project, instead create your own VPC.

A VPC can have public and private subnets. Only the public facing component, the load balancer in your architecture, should be in public subnets. All other resources - EC2 instances, auto-scaling groups, RDS instances, Memcached nodes - should be in private subnets. Apply the principle of least privileges, if a resource does not need to be open to the Internet, deploy it in private subnets.

Apply the principle of security in depth, use multiple security measures. The default security group is configured to allow unrestricted flow - all protocols, all ports - between servers that use the same security group. You used the same security group for all tiers in your architecture, so effectively any server can connect to any other server in the architecture using any protocol or port.

This goes against the principle of least privileges. Don't use the default security group, instead create a security group for each tier - one each for the load balancer, the app server, the RDS instances, and the Memcached cluster. Each security group must restrict access only to the required protocol, port, and the source. For instance, configure inbound rules such that only the app servers can connect to RDS instances, and only using the MySQL protocol and port.

DynamoDB is available only over the Internet. Your app servers running in private subnets will not be able to connect to DynamoDB because private subnets are isolated from the Internet. You will need to use a VPC service endpoint to get around this problem, the service endpoint opens up a private connection between your private subnets and the DynamoDB service. The service endpoint can also be used from public subnets, this way, your network costs can be lowered.

It is a good idea to restrict actions and resources that can be accessed via the VPC service endpoint. You can do this by configuring, with your VPC service endpoint, a custom policy, much like the IAM policy used in an earlier chapter.

## Implementation

You will now create a VPC with two public and two private subnets. You will create DB subnet groups for RDS and the Memcached cluster, these groups should include just the private subnets. You will create multiple security groups, one each for the Elastic Load Balancer, the web servers, the database servers and the Memcached cluster. Finally, you will create a VPC service endpoint for DynamoDB, so that your app can connect to the DynamoDB table without having to go to the Internet.

Here are is some things to note before you get started:

### VPC Wizard
The VPC wizard is a tool that helps creates VPCs easily. It supports four simple VPC configurations or scenarios. You

will use the wizard to create a scenario 1 VPC. You will then modify this VPC, by hand, in subsequent steps.

### New subnets are private
When you create a new subnet manually, it is created as a private subnet. If you need a public subnet, you will need to change the route table of the subnet, change to the route table that has an Internet Gateway configured in it.

### Subnet IP address ranges
The IP address ranges in your subnets must be distinct, so that there is no IP address conflict. Use the following ranges for the four subnets you will create: 10.0.0.0/24 (this is the default value in the VPC wizard), 10.0.1.0/24, 10.0.2.0/24, and 10.0.3.0/24.

### Nested security groups
In most of your security groups rules, you will use other security groups as the source. When you do this, requests will be restricted to servers that use that security group. For instance, in your database security group, you will set the source to be the security group used by your app servers, this would restrict database access only to your app servers.

### Db subnet groups
You will create subnet groups for your RDS instances and for your Memcached cluster. The subnet group is a way to configure which subnets the nodes will come up in. You should ensure that the database subnet groups only have private subnets in them.

### CREATE VIRTUAL PRIVATE CLOUD

Figure 8.2: VPC wizard with scenario 1 selected

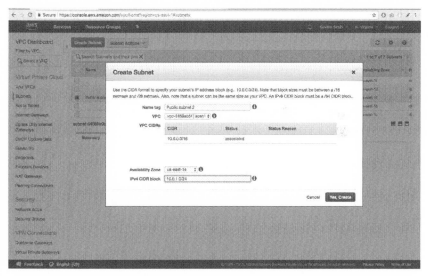

Figure 8:3: Adding a VPC subnet

Figure 8.4: Change subnets' route table to make subnet public

1. Use the VPC wizard and create a VPC as follows:

---

**VPC scenario**
Select the first scenario.

**VPC IP address range**
Leave unchanged at the default value of 10.0.0.0/16.

**Subnet IP address range**
Leave unchanged at the default value of 10.0.0.0/24.

**Subnet zone**
Select a zone, say 1a.

**Other Configurations**
Use default values.

---

2. After the VPC is created, add a second public subnet, manually, as follows:

**Subnet zone**
Select a different zone, say 1b.

**Subnet IP address range**
Set to 10.0.1.0/24.

**Other Configurations**
Use default values.

3. Change the route table of this new subnet, so it becomes a public subnet. By default, new subnets are created as private subnets. The VPC will have two route tables, one for public subnets (table has an Internet Gateway configured) and one for private subnets (table does not have the Internet Gateway configured). Configure the subnet to use the route table that has an Internet Gateway.

4. Add a private subnet to the VPC:

**Subnet zone**
Choose zone 1a (same as the first public subnet's zone).

**Subnet IP address range**
Set to 10.0.2.0/24.

**Other Configurations**
Use default values.

5. Add a second private subnet:

**Subnet zone**
Choose zone 1b (same as the second public subnet's zone).

**Subnet IP address range**
Set to 10.0.3.0/24.

**Other Configurations**
Use default values.

6. Verify the setup:
* Public subnets should be in different availability zones - 1a and 1b.
* Private subnets should also be in different zones - 1a and 1b.
* Public subnets' route table should have the Internet Gateway.
* Private subnets' route table should not have the Internet Gateway.

## CONFIGURE NESTED SECURITY GROUPS

Figure 8.5: Set security group Id as the source

1. Create a security group for the load balancer as follows:

> **Inbound rule**
> Allow HTTP (port 80) requests, set the source to 'anywhere' (0.0.0.0/0).

2. Create a security group for the app layer as follows:

> **Inbound rule**
> Allow HTTP (port 80) requests, configure the source as the load balancer's security group.

3. Create a security group for the Memcached cluster:

> **Inbound rule**
> Allow TCP (port 11211) requests, configure the source as the app layer's security group.

4. Create a security group for the RDS instances:

> **Inbound rule**
> Allow MySQL (port 3306) requests, configure the source as the app layer's security group.

**CREATE DB SUBNET GROUPS**

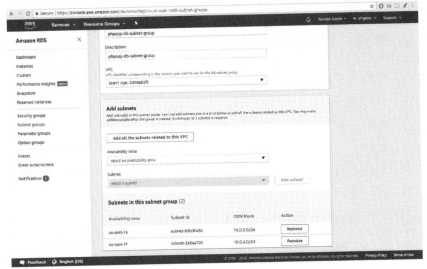

Figure 8.6: Include only private subnets in Db subnet groups

1. Create a subnet group in RDS that includes only the private subnets created above.
2. Create a Memcached subnet group in ElastiCache that includes only the private subnets created above.

## CREATE VPC SERVICE ENDPOINT FOR DYNAMODB

Figure 8.7: Configure the VPC service endpoint for both public and private subnets

1. Create a DynamoDB service endpoint for your VPC as follows:

---

**VPC**
Select your VPC.

**Configure route tables**
Select both route tables of your VPC.

**Custom policy**
Configure a custom policy as provided below.
```
{
  "Version": "2008-10-17",
    "Statement": [
      {
        "Sid": "AccessToSpecificTable",
        "Effect": "Allow",
        "Principal": "*",
        "Action": [
          "dynamodb:GetItem",
          "dynamodb:PutItem",
          "dynamodb:Update*"
        ],
        "Resource":
"arn:aws:dynamodb:us-east-1:*:table/sessions"
      }
    ]
}
```

---

**VERIFY NETWORK SETUP**
1. Launch an RDS instance in this new VPC, use the DB subnet group created earlier.

2. Launch a Memcached cluster, use the DB subnet group created earlier.
3. Launch an EC2 instance in the public subnet of this VPC.
4. Configure the RDS and Memcached cluster endpoints in the PHP app.
5. Test the application using the EC2 instance's public IP address. Verify that the DynamoDB sessions, RDS, and Memcached pages work as expected.

# CHAPTER 9: CAPSTONE

## Introduction

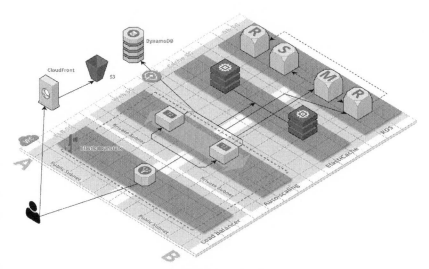

Figure 9.1: Capstone

**Objectives**
You now have all the knowledge, and all the skills you need, to build a complete, fault-tolerant, scalable, secure and easy to deploy stack. In this chapter, you will combine, sometimes in new ways, all the individual elements and ideas from the previous chapters, to build the architecture shown in the figure above. Think of this chapter as a capstone project that you will do on your own, this chapter does not include any implementation steps.

**You will learn about**
Multi-AZ read replicas, multi-node Memcached clusters, load-balanced and auto-scaled Elastic Beanstalk environments, and VPC NAT Gateways.

# Discussion

You have practiced, in previous chapters, most of what you need to do here. Here is a list of things that you will do for the first time in this chapter:

* Implement a load balanced and auto-scaled Beanstalk environment. In chapter 7, you created a single instance Beanstalk environment.

* Configure the Beanstalk environment's auto-scaling group in private subnets. In chapter 7, your Beanstalk environment was in a public subnet.

* Configure two nodes in the Memcached cluster, distributed across two availability zones. This is fault-tolerant. In chapter 5, you created a single node cluster.

* Create a multi-AZ RDS read replica, again for fault-tolerance. In chapter 5, you created a single read replica instance.

* Configure the VPC service endpoint for DynamoDB to be available to the private subnets only. Your auto-scaling group will be in private subnets, the service endpoint is not needed in the public subnets. In chapter 9, you configured the service endpoint for both the route tables of your VPC, which means the VPC service endpoint was available to both public and private subnets.

# Implementation

This chapter has no implementation steps, but here are a couple of quick tips on setting up a load-balanced, auto-scaled Beanstalk environment, when using public and private subnets, and when using nested security groups:

**Security groups**

When creating the Beanstalk environment, you will not be able to configure separate security groups for the load balancer and for the auto-scaling group. Specify the load balancer's security group, Beanstalk will automatically create a security group for the auto-scaling group. Configure this security group as the source in your database security groups.

## NAT gateway

Beanstalk needs Internet access to function properly. Beanstalk will not be able to create the auto-scaling group in private subnets unless the private subnets are configured with a NAT gateway. The NAT gateway allows private subnets to access the Internet on the outbound side.

# SUMMARY

In this book, you have learned about these AWS services - EC2, EBS, RDS, S3, DynamoDB, IAM, ElastiCache, CloudFront, Elastic Beanstalk and VPC.

You now understand these important aspects of AWS:
* Infrastructure: AWS Regions and AWS Availability Zones.
* EC2: Amazon Machine Images, EBS snapshots, Application Load Balancers, Sticky Sessions, Auto-Scaling Groups.
* RDS: Read Replicas, Multi-AZ Deployment.
* Network: Public and Private Subnets, VPC Service Endpoints, Security Groups, NAT Gateways.
* Security: IAM Roles, IAM policies, S3 bucket policies, CloudFront signed URLs.
* App development: AWS SDK.

You also understand these best practices:
* Configure separate root and data EBS volumes.
* Regularly snapshot EBS data volumes.
* Regularly create Amazon Machine Images of your app servers.
* Use multiple instances and multiple zones.
* Centralize sessions, content and the database.
* Use auto-scaling groups for your app or web servers.
* Off-load database requests to read replicas or to in-memory databases.
* Use a Content Distribution Network to deliver content to users around the world.
* Use signed URLs to deliver private content.
* Configure security using the principle of least privileges.
* Use an automation platform for frequent deployments.

You also understand AWS best practices for typical app functions:
* Sessions: centralize sessions in DynamoDB.
* Database: separate into RDS tier, use ElastiCache and RDS read replicas for scalability.
* Content: Use S3 for storage and CloudFront for distribution. Use Signed URLs for security.

# BOOK REVIEW

Book reviews make a huge difference, I will really appreciate it if you can leave one for this book on Amazon. Thank you.

# OTHER AWS BOOKS

AWS CERTIFIED CLOUD PRACTITIONER (CLF-C01) EXAM - PRACTICE TESTS: 2 PRACTICE TESTS (25 QUESTIONS EACH), BY SAVITRA SIROHI
https://www.amazon.com/dp/B07QCCCB5T

AWS CERTIFIED SOLUTIONS ARCHITECT ASSOCIATE (SAA-CO1) EXAM - PRACTICE TESTS: 2 PRACTICE TESTS (25 QUESTIONS EACH), BY SAVITRA SIROHI
https://www.amazon.com/dp/B07R7G862H

AWS CERTIFIED SYSOPS ADMINISTRATOR ASSOCIATE (SOA-C01) EXAM - PRACTICE TESTS: 2 PRACTICE TESTS (20 QUESTIONS EACH), BY SAVITRA SIROHI
https://www.amazon.com/dp/B07RK68267

Made in the USA
Columbia, SC
19 July 2019